MW00352945

Hunny Bunny

Hunny Bunny

A little book about friendship

by

Melissa Masters

Copyright © Melissa Masters

ISBN 10: 1-58790-574-4

ISBN 13: 978-1-58790-574-2

Library of Congress Catalog Number: 2021935818

Manufactured in the U.S.A.
REGENT PRESS
Berkeley, California
www.regentpress.net

for you ♡

Melissa Masters
♡

Urban Dictionary:

Hunny -bunny

This is a nickname said to someone you like,
love, or is very sweet.

Visiting Day

In the morning Hunny Bunny
woke up and ate a carrot.

He exercised.

He read an interesting book.

Hunny Bunny played dress up,

and painted a colorful picture.

In the afternoon he went
to visit friends.

He met Beetle.

They played the
Looking Close game.

He saw Snake
in the meadow.

They played the
Slithering game.

Hunny Bunny said
hello to Frog.

They played the
Jumping game.

As the sun disappeared,

he noticed Owl.

They played the
Staring game.

Hunny Bunny arrived home
and ate a carrot.

He said a prayer of
gratitude for the day,

and then ....ZZzzzz.

A Best Buddy

Hunny Bunny and Squirrel
were good friends yet
each had very
different interests.

Hunny Bunny enjoyed exploring in the
vegetable garden,
while Squirrel preferred
to climb trees.

Squirrel loved making his
friend laugh by twirling
in circles to
chase his tail.

One day Hunny Bunny
watched unamused.
"Why is your tail so big
and fluffy, and mine so
small?" said Hunny Bunny.

Squirrel looked directly at
his friend and replied,
"Well, why are your ears
so long and smooth,
and mine so little?"

The friends thought about
this and then smiled.
"We are each unique!"
Hunny Bunny exclaimed.

Suddenly Squirrel
propped up his
tail, and Hunny
Bunny made his ears
stand straight.

They began to giggle.
Before long they were
rolling in the grass...

and racing across the yard.

All Together

Autumn leaves swirled under a full moon in early November. The animals hurried to their meeting place beside a large oak tree in the Thompson's backyard.

44

Hunny Bunny's hat blew right off, and Racoon quickly
retrieved it.

Skunk spoke first.

"Let's call this meeting to order,

as it is

quite chilly!"

The Mouse family listened intently,
father eager to find
supper in the garden.

Snake wiggled impatiently
while two feral kittens
pawed her gingerly.

Rat climbed onto a rock to speak in his loudest voice. "The annual election for governor of this yard will begin after a few final words from our candidates."

Owl, perched high on a branch, announced how she would make sure that all the animals are treated with respect. She spread her wings and let out a bellowing hoot.

Chipmunk proclaimed the need for everyone to take responsibility in caring for the environment so they all can thrive. He meandered through the crowd before resting on a tree stump grinning proudly.

Rat continued, "You will each get an acorn to place in this shallow hole. Acorns with tops are a vote for Owl, acorns with tops removed will go to Chipmunk. Let's begin!"

Squirrel carried his vote promptly to the hole. Goose asked for assistance from Snake in removing her acorn top. Hunny Bunny and Turtle pondered their decision.

By the time stars appeared brighter,
the voting was complete.
Racoon and Opossum
counted the tally.

Raccoon handed Rat
the final result,
then looked at
Opossum and shrugged.

The animals huddled closer, anxious to hear the winning name. "This is unbelievable," stammered Rat.
"We have a tie!"

A hushed silence broke into exuberant cheers. Owl and Chipmunk agreed to cooperate together as they all danced merrily in the moonlight.

Hunny Bunny and his friends soon dashed home. They were glad that the Thompson yard was a most harmonious place to live...

Food for Thought
and we can all choose to get along . . .

also,
carrots make a healthy snack.

The end.

The muse for this book was a stuffed rabbit I fashioned from my dad's old socks. In memoriam of my dear dad, and sweet mom who often called her offspring "hunny-bunnies." M.M.

Melissa Masters lives in
Northern California where nature
inspires and delights.
Visit: www.yourlifeisamasterpiece.com
for more information about
her creative work.

CPSIA information can be obtained
at www.ICGtesting.com
Printed in the USA
JSHW010313170621
15974JS00002B/4

9 781587 905742